The *dream* BIG Bitches

VISION BOOK

BRANDEN LANETTE
Dreamer-In-Chief

Published by

SUCCESS IN

P·A·G·E·S

SHORT BOOKS. BIG IDEAS.

www.SuccessIn100Pages.com

ISBN 978-1-947814-81-3

Copyright © Branden LaNette

2020

DEDICATION:

This workbook is dedicated to you, the league of bitches with whom I find strength and solace. If life gives you a chance, take it. If it doesn't, make one of your own.

REQUIRED WARNING:

As with my book, *Once Upon a Time, Bitches,* this workbook contains a fair amount of *spicy* language, coupled with a healthy dose of brutal honesty. Personally, I wanted to ditch the foul language, but my publisher insisted I keep being myself—you know, authenticity, and all that. So, buckle-up, prepare yourself for some strong advice, strong language, and try not to be too fucking offended. Okay?

-Branden LaNette

(while breastfeeding my youngest and scooping rabbit shit at 2:47 a.m.)

What's In This Thing?

Part I:

Introduction: About This Workbook

Part II:

The Power of Visualization

Part III:

Getting Clarity on What You Want

Part IV:

What Are You Willing to Do to Get It?

Part V:

What Are You Willing to Stop Doing?

Part VI:

Identifying Self-Limiting Beliefs

Part VII:

Operating From a Place of Gratitude

"PEOPLE WITH INTEGRITY DO WHAT
THEY SAY THEY ARE GOING TO DO.
OTHERS HAVE EXCUSES."

–DR. LAURA SCHLESSINGER

Okay, ditch
the excuses.
Got it!

PART I:

Introduction: About This Workbook

I hope you're not allergic to rolling up your sleeves, because we've got a bit of work to do!

First Off, Who The Fuck Am I?

Let's get this straight: this Vision Book is all about YOU. But since I'm the bitch who wants to help you, you need to know who the hell I am so we can form some trust, and so you'll do the work I'm going to ask you to do.

Hopefully, you've read my book, *Once Upon a Time, Bitches*. If not, you should. It provides the foundation for this book. And I like money.

As you may have seen on the cover, I don't look like a typical author. But I have long ignored what people say I should say, do, or look like. My name is Branden, a boy's name bestowed on me by my jerk-ass mother, a woman who couldn't find an ounce of kindness inside her with a map and a flashlight. The only things my mother and I have in common are droopy boobs, stretch marks, and…

Nope, that's it.

> *Don't worry about making others believe in your dreams. Focus on making sure YOU believe in them.*

I ended up on my own at a very young age, with the wrong guy, the wrong jobs, making all the wrong choices and going nowhere fast. The fairytale I was promised as a child never materialized. That's when it hit me: Prince Charming wasn't coming to save me. I would have to save myself.

I also realized that accepting your life is fucked up is only half the battle—*the other half is figuring out what you want instead.*

What did I want? I wanted happiness (duh), an interesting word that's easy to throw around but harder to define. Specifically, I wanted to be in a loving relationship with someone who I could count on to support me no matter what.

Knowing this, I left a destructive relationship and made room for this person to arrive in my life, and he did. I found my Prince Charming.

Next, I knew I wanted to be a Mom, more accurately, a good one. To date I've created six wonderful C-section babies who now span in age from toddler to young adult. Along with my Prince, they are the joys of my life.

Next on my fairytale wish list was my dream of becoming a published author. I go into more detail on this in my book, but for our purposes here let it suffice to say I have been able to put a check mark next to that one, too.

Now I'm working on building my business as an entrepreneur, coach, and professional speaker. In short, my life is finally unfolding exactly the way I planned it.

Don't get me wrong, it's been no "pleasure cruise" (to quote Freddie Mercury.) It's been "a long and winding road" (to quote Paul McCartney.) There's been plenty of struggle, but along the way I managed to stay focused on what I wanted rather than what I didn't want. One by one, I set goals and got busy working on them. I never gave up, because 'when you wish upon a star…' (no book about manifesting your fairytale life would be complete without a Disney song, right? Okay, no more song lyrics, I promise.)

The Focus of <u>This</u> Workbook

In *Once Upon a Time, Bitches,* I introduced my Seven Magical Maxims for living a fairytale life. And while all the maxims are important, *this* book is focused almost exclusively on **Maxim #4…**

> **Dream dreams that are so BIG they make people doubt you.**

Because everything starts with a dream.

As I shared in my book, I am a compulsive dreamer. My dreams have always been there, always been with me. I can remember no inciting incident where suddenly my dreams were kindled. They have simply *been there,* like standard options on a vehicle. And I'm pretty sure I'm not alone.

Chances are good, since you are holding this workbook in your hands, you and I are the same. We both have fantasies of living the good life. We both want to do great things with our lives.

When it comes to dreams, let me be clear—I am not interested in dreams for the sake of dreaming—I want the damn things to come true! And once I reach one goal, I set my sights on more goals. Goals that are bigger and better.

If I told you all the things that were on my dream list, you'd think I was fucking crazy. My dreams are far past any idea of what's normal, I know that. But they're *my* dreams, and nobody can tell me I can't have them. I give birth to dreams almost as fast as I give birth to children.

Executing <u>Your</u> Dreams

When it comes to making dreams come true, it's all about execution, bitches. Trust me, I know. I've tried simply *'wishin' and hopin' and thinkin' and prayin'* (shit, another song reference), and that got me nowhere. I discovered there's a formula for making your dreams come to pass and dreaming is only half of the process. The other half is doing the fucking work. Even prayer has its limits.

Face it, bitches—God is busy doing a lot of other shit.

So, when it comes to getting new shoes, a sports car, your dream home, God wants you to get off your ass and make an effort. Every time I ask God for something, I just imagine her saying: *"Hey, bitch, my hands are full right now, can I get a little help here?"*

When it comes to achieving my dreams, I am in a perpetual state of action. I push for them constantly. My goals and dreams are more important to me than water. What about you? What dreams do you have? How big are your dreams?

Alan Watts said, *"You can't get wet from the word water."* Brilliant. If you want to achieve big dreams, you've got to be willing to jump in, get wet, and paddle your ass off. So this is *not* a 'think about it book'… it's a <u>work</u>book, bitches! A place to start the process of *doing the work.* So if you want to get a return on your investment, I hope you're willing to roll up your Lululemon's and sweat a bit.

Do You Want to Know a Secret?

Chances are good you've seen the personal development movie, *The Secret*. At a minimum

I get the feeling Branden is expecting a lot from us, don't you?

you've heard of it and know it's about the Law of Attraction, which in a sentence suggests you get in life what you think about and focus on. The truth is…

There is no fucking secret.

Am I dissing *The Secret*? Hell, no.

The Secret is one of the most important personal development messages all time, getting the Law Of Attraction to the masses in a big, big way. And, for the record, I totally believe in the LOA—and this workbook proves it. The point I'm trying to make is: *The Secret* isn't a secret. It never was.

People want you to *think* there is some big secret in order to make it sound exotic and mysterious. It's simply great marketing—new packaging of an old idea.

People have been talking about the **L- O-A… F-O-R-E-V-E-R.** Just look at the following quotes from some of the world's most well-known (and really old) people:

"Our life is what our thoughts make it."
-Marcus Aurelius

"What you think you become. What you feel you attract. What you imagine you create."
-Buddha

"A man is but the product of his thoughts. What he thinks he becomes."
– Gandhi

"Whatever the mind can conceive it can achieve."
– W. Clement Stone

"Imagination is everything. It is the preview of life's coming attractions." – Albert Einstein

And just in case Einstein's endorsement of the Law of Attraction doesn't convince you, there's always Willie Nelson:

"Once you replace negative thoughts with positive ones, you'll start having positive results."
– Willie Nelson

And if Willie Nelson hasn't turned you into a believer, there's always that famous DJ, Mark in the Morning (on K-GOD) who said:

"What things so-ever ye desire, when ye pray, believe that ye receive them, and ye shall have them," **(Mark 11:24)** *and "If thou can believe, all things are possible, to him that believeth."* **(Mark 9:23)**

In short, if the Law of Attraction is a secret, it's the worst kept fucking secret in history!

Why Aren't <u>You</u> Using the LOA?

If *The Secret* isn't really a secret, why in the hell aren't you using it already? (Or, if you *are* using it, why aren't you using it better and more often?) This is not a rhetorical question, bitches—I really want to know.

Circle the answer(s) below that apply to you:

A) *You've been living under a rock and never heard of it before.*

B) *You've heard of it, but you don't believe in "touchy-feely woo-woo stuff."*

C) *You heard of it AND believe in it, but you've been too busy to try it.*

D) *You tried it once, but–just like your New Year's Eve resolutions—you gave up on it in a few days.*

E) *Insert some other fucking-lame excuse here.*

Hey, don't get me wrong, I'm not perfect when it comes to all this stuff—I don't have *everything* I want, and I've only scratched the surface of what I'm capable of achieving.

But the things I *have* achieved are in large part due to the Law of Attraction and the use of vision boards. And the results have blown my mind.

What if I told you the universe is conspiring behind your back to help you become successful? Well, it is.

"NEVER LET PEOPLE WITH SMALL MINDS CONVINCE YOU THAT YOUR DREAMS ARE TOO BIG. IF YOUR DREAMS WEREN'T POSSIBLE, YOU WOULDN'T HAVE THEM."

–BRANDEN LANETTE

Sometimes the people with the biggest brains have the smallest minds!

PART II:

The Power of Visualization

The Power of "Visioning"

Vision boards (also referred to as a dream boards) are a collection of thoughts and pictures that represent the goals and dreams you want to achieve. They're central to using the Law of Attraction effectively.

In this case, you're creating a *vision book,* a portable version of a full-sized vision board that can be placed on your desk, in your bag when you go to work, or slid in your luggage when you travel.

Of course, there's nothing stopping you from creating a large vision board, too. Having pictures on your wall that you can see all day is the way most people do it. I think you should have both.

Jack Canfield, co-author of the "Chicken Soup for the Soul®" book series and "The Success Principles" says:

> *"Your brain will work tirelessly to achieve the statements you give your subconscious mind. And when those statements are the affirmations and images of your goals, you are destined to achieve them."*

I don't know Jack (not personally, at least), but I follow his work and trust the shit out of the man. And if he says vision boards work, you should believe him, too.

Like most topics, I only understand it enough to be dangerous. As such, I have no intention of digging deeply into the science behind the Law of Attraction—I simply know it works. Like gravity and electricity, you don't have to understand the science behind *why* they work and *how* they work—you just have to be smart enough to plug your hair dryer in, and not dumb enough to jump off a tall building.

Here's just a little background so you're sold on the idea…

Hey, if visualization works the way you say it does Branden, then count me in!

Understanding the R.A.S.

When you create a vision board, you're telling your brain, *"Hey, this is what I want."* And when you do this, you activate a mechanism in the brain called the Reticular Activating System— also known as the RAS (pronounced, RAZ)—a network of neurons located in the brain stem. This not only allows your brain to focus on what you've told it you want, but it helps the brain *screen out* the millions of other unimportant things it *could* be focused on.

For example, this is why when you buy a new car—say, a Lexus RX350—you start seeing Lexus RX350s everywhere you look. I mean everywhere. Where in the hell were all these RX350s before? They were everywhere, but your brain simply wasn't looking for them.

Before, they were screened out by your mind, and now they're not.

And it's the same with your goals. You tell your brain what you want, and your brain starts looking for ways to get it. Why? Because that's it's fucking job, bitches! The brain is a problem-solving machine, the greatest ever created. But you have to tell your brain what the problem is that what you want solved—*that's your job.*

The RAS also seeks information that validates your beliefs. For example, tell your brain that you're awesome, and it looks for proof that validates your awesomeness. Isn't that fucking awesome?

On the other hand, tell your brain that you suck, it will start searching for proof that validates *that.* This is why negative self-talk is so destructive.

Oh, I get it— to 'visualize' is to create visual-LIES!

Right, visual-Lies that eventually become visual-TRUTHS!

Repetitive Visualization Is Critical to Goal Achievement

As I pointed out in *Once Upon a Time, Bitches*, merely creating a vision board or vision book doesn't mean shit unless you use it. You've got to do more than simply cutting out and pasting pictures. Take the time to focus, visualize and internalize your goals and dreams. How often?

Every damn day, bitches.

Twice a day is better.

I sit in front of my vision board for 10 minutes every morning and 10 minutes at night, right before I go to sleep (hence the term, *dream board*.) And when you visualize, you should visualize things as if they have already come true. Make no mistake—vision boards are some powerful shit and not to be taken lightly.

The things you focus on intensely and consistently *are* going to come about. Trust me, *they are.* Maybe not today, or even tomorrow— *but eventually.* So don't fuck around, bitches. Take the process seriously.

Here are a few things to keep in mind:

1... Be Specific and Selective

When putting pictures into your Vision Book, only include pictures of things you *really want*— things that will make you *truly happy. Be* selective. Don't clutter your vision book with day to day crap, like a toaster oven. If you do, it dilutes your focus and reduces your chances of getting the things that *really matter* to you.

2... Make Sure Everything Is What <u>You</u> Want

> *Everything is created twice, once in the imagination, and then in physical reality.*

Your vision book should be a collection of thoughts and images that reflect *your* goals and dreams, not things other people want or expect from you. And when you're done, it should be something so special and powerful that if you lost it, you'd be sick, as if someone had stolen a map to hidden treasure..

Because that's what the Vision Book really is— a *photo album of your future life.* Right now it's only an imagined future, but with enough focus and emotion, thoughts become things. Make sure the things you put in your vision book are the right things.

3... Write in the "Present Tense"

When possible try to write in the present tense, and again, be specific. Don't say, *"I want to be wealthy."* Instead, say "I am wealthy." Better still, be specific. "I earn $300,000 per year, have $100,000 in savings, and my total net worth is $1,000,000."

When you say things like, "I wish I was in a loving relationship," your brain says, "Oh, how nice, a wish." But when you say, "I am in a loving relationship with someone who is kind, caring and driven (specific), your brain says, "Oh, this is a directive that must be fulfilled." Big difference.

4... Identify Your "Why" for Everything You Want

There is a *why* behind every single thing we want, so I've included prompts to remind you to *acknowledge your why* for that particular item. The more reasons you can identify, the more likely you are to get what you want.

This is important. If the box provided is too small for your list of reasons, use additional paper.

And, finally...

5... Do the Fucking Exercises

I'd like to think it's not necessary to say this, but I will anyway: Do the fucking exercises. No, really. I mean *really.* Really do the exercises. All of them. No exceptions.

I know you want to skip them. Everyone does. It's human nature to simply read and quickly move along. Don't.

If you want your **BIG DREAMS** to come true, you've got to take the process seriously. And that's why you bought this book right—to achieve big dreams? So, no shortcuts! Write you answers in the damn book, cut out the damn pictures, and do your daily visualizations.

All the best...

Branden

P.S. WARNING: DO NOT USE MARKERS OR "SHARPIES!"

Don't use markers/Sharpies! They bleed through the paper and make it hard to read what's on the other side.

"IF YOU HAVE BUILT CASTLES IN THE AIR, YOUR WORK NEED NOT BE LOST; THAT IS WHERE THEY SHOULD BE. NOW PUT THE FOUNDATIONS UNDER THEM."

—HENRY DAVID THOREAU

PART III:

Getting Clarity on What You Want

I hope there's a lot of room to write goals and paste pictures in here—my wish list is kinda long!

What kind of WORK do I really want to

DO...

We all have a dream job, a dream career, every one of us. But few of us ever live that dream. You tell your parents you want to be a dancer, and they say, *"Oh, you can't make a living at that! You should get a real job—why don't you be a lawyer?"* It's all about playing it safe. But what if playing it safe is the riskiest thing you can do? What if the most logical thing is to pursue *your* dream? Think about it: what are you most likely to quit doing—something you hate doing or something you love? Jim Carrey says you can fail at something you hate, so you might as well fail at something you love. For me, that thing is writing. What is it for you? Don't blame the universe for not delivering something if you've never bothered asking for it!

Describe Your Dream Work Here...

> My dream is to work from home and make money online so I can spend more time with my kids!

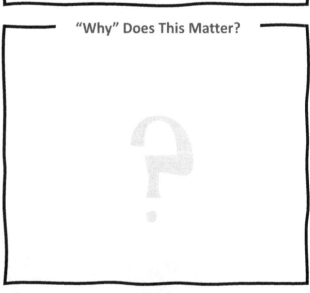

"Why" Does This Matter?

Place Pictures Here

What kind of LOVING RELATIONSHIP do I want to
ENJOY...

Not only can you have the relationship of your dreams but let's get one important thing out of the way, bitches: *you deserve it.* You deserve to trust and to be trusted, respected, adored, and loved.

I get it. I was on the road to settling for what I *thought* was good enough, until I came to my senses and changed my mind about what a dream partner was supposed to be.

Who, exactly, do you want to spend the rest of your life with? Now, I'm not suggesting you run out and get divorced or ditch your present partner (note: I'm not responsible for that shit/please see disclaimer) but if you're unhappy—and especially if you're experiencing abuse—get the fuck out, bitch. And in case you think that special someone doesn't exist for you, think again. They do. Finding them starts with creating a clear picture as to who they are in your mind.

Describe Your Dream Partner Here...

"Why" Is This Important?

Hmmm... what kind of dream partner do I want to attract? Well, let's start with...

Place Pictures Here

What things do I want to
ACHIEVE...

It's time to take a minute to consider what types of things you want to achieve in your life. Maybe it's winning one of the most-well-known awards, like: the Pulitzer Prize, a Nobel Prize, an Oscar, a Grammy, an Olympic medal, etc. Or maybe you're reading this while you're still in school and you want to win a State Championship, or an NCAA title in your chosen sport. Or to become the class valedictorian. Or maybe there's no "award" attached, like climbing Mt. Everest.

People's goals change over time, of course. My first goal was to write a book. Then it became to get it published. Then it was to hit a best-seller list. Then it became getting a second book published (clue: it's in your hand.) So, knowing your goals will change, what are the goals you've set your sights on right now?

List Your Desired Achievements Here...

This might sound crazy, but I really want to get my PhD in psychology!

"Why" Would Achieving This Matter?

Place Pictures Here

WHERE do I want to
LIVE...

Let's take a drone's eye view and ask, where do you want to live? What city and state? In an urban area or in a rural landscape dotted with barns and cows? Another country entirely, perhaps?

Pretend your house was picked up by a *Wizard of Oz* tornado and you could have it dropped *(ever so gently, 'Good Witch' style)* anywhere you wanted. The choice is entirely yours. *"But, Branden, have a job, I can't move. My family lives here. I'm trapped!"* I agree—with an attitude like that, you are trapped!

I'm not saying it will be easy. There will be hurdles to jump. Turn the challenge over to your subconscious and let it find the possibilities. That's what it's good at!

I can live anywhere I want to? That's fucking awesome!

List Your Dream Place to Live Here...

"Why" There?

Place Pictures Here

What is my
DREAM HOUSE....

I'm not psychic but I am betting that you are not living in your "dream house" yet, and if you *are*—congratulations! And if that's the case, maybe this exercise will give you some inspiration for a remodel! In any case, dreaming about your dream house is some of the most motivational dreaming you can do.

When I'm dreaming about my dream house, I usually start from the outside, as I imagine most people do. Is your dream house a mansion, castle, log cabin, townhouse, or country farmhouse? Or maybe it's a penthouse condo with floor to ceiling windows, or a tree house. From there, I imagine walking in the front door and going from room to room, designing every inch and aspect of what each room looks like.

Finally, I look out the windows from the inside and take in the view of everything that surrounds it. Do it any way you want but do it. There are dream pages for every room to follow.

"Why" Do I Want This?

There are no limits here, it's your dream house, so dream!

House Exterior

Place Pictures Here

View

Place Pictures Here

BRANDEN LANETTE

Living Room

Place Pictures Here

Furniture

Place Pictures Here

BRANDEN LANETTE

Dining Room

Place Pictures Here

Bedroom

Place Pictures Here

BRANDEN LANETTE

Kitchen

Place Pictures Here

Bathroom

Place Pictures Here

BRANDEN LANETTE

Closet

Place Pictures Here

Place Pictures Here

BRANDEN LANETTE

Garage

Place Pictures Here

Game Room

Place Pictures Here

BRANDEN LANETTE

Other

things you may want, like a workout room, cigar room,
media room, wine cellar, deck, kid's room(s), etc.

Place Pictures Here

Other

things you may want, like a workout room, cigar room,
media room, wine cellar, deck, kid's room(s), etc.

Place Pictures Here

BRANDEN LANETTE

Other

things you may want, like a workout room, cigar room,
media room, wine cellar, deck, kid's room(s), etc.

Place Pictures Here

What level of FITNESS do I want to REACH...

The reasons for being physically fit are too obvious to mention, but let's list them anyway:

- More confidence
- Better sleep
- More energy
- Greater productivity
- Look better, feel better
- Better mental health
- Fewer health problems
- Ability to handle stress

Did I miss anything? Oh, yeah—and you won't motherfucking die!

So help me God, bitches, if I have to give you more reasons to get your ass into the gym, we're in trouble.

Oh, wait, there *are* two more:

1… Because you love yourself, and…

2… Because I care about you, too!

Describe Your Ideal Level of Fitness Here…

"Why" Is This Important?

GET DOWN AND GIVE ME TWENTY!!!

Place Pictures Here

What IMAGE do I want to PROJECT...

Let's face it, most of us would rather ask the Fairy Godmother to whip up some super soft pajamas in place of the sparkly ball gown—at least that's the way it is for me. But while it's fun to be comfortable in private, it's critical to take conscious control over the image we project in public which affects the perception people have about us. About our age, success, likeability, education level, health, and on and on.

"Wait a minute, Branden, one minute you say we shouldn't care about what other people think of us, now you're saying we need to control our image. What gives?"

What gives is, you're not controlling your image for them—you're controlling it for *you*. Because people DO make snap judgements about us, it's important that their judgements help us achieve *our* goals.

What Image Do I Want to Project?

"Why" Should I Care?

Place Pictures Here

What kind of KICKASS CAR(s) do I want to
DRIVE?

Here's the thing about owning a kickass car—it's simply not a Vision Book without one! Right?

Let me caution you here, though: no one needs to have a kickass car, like a Lamborghini Diablo or my dream car, the Mercedes AMG-GT. And while a sports car isn't a must have, it's one hell of a fucking great bonus! And since the universe is giving them out…

But don't let my dreams be yours. Don't cut out pictures of the sports cars you hear other people saying are their dream—focus on the car of your *dreams*. If you're the type of person who doesn't give a rats-ass about sports cars, then skip this page. Or if it's 9-passenger minivan that floats your boat, put *that* picture in the book. NEVER want something because other people want it—want it because YOU want it!

Describe Your Dream Car(s) Here...

"Why" Do I Want This?

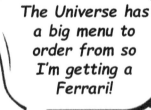

The Universe has a big menu to order from so I'm getting a Ferrari!

Place Pictures Here

What "ART" do I want to
CREATE...

When you hear the word art, what's the first thing that pops in your mind? Most people answer *painting.* Some answer *sculpture.* Others say *music, film* and *dance.* The truth is, anything can be elevated to the level of art:

For some people, decorating cakes is an art—*for other's, it's merely a job.* For some people, designing logos is an art—*for others it's a paycheck. For some people, m*aking jewelry is an art—*for others, it's just a way to make a living.* Cooking is art for lots of people—*for others it's making dinner.* Delivering the perfect speech can be art—*for others it's a fate worse than death!*

Whether something is "art" depends on your perception of it, and how much of yourself you're willing to pour into it..

List the "Art" You Want to Make...

"Why" Do I Want This?

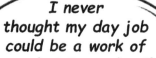

> I never thought my day job could be a work of art—but it can be if I want it to be!

Place Pictures Here

Where do I want to
TRAVEL...

We are doing some deep work in this Vision Book, but you've got to admit it's pretty damn fun because it's about experiencing the world, bitches! Now, the question is: *Where do you want to go?* I mean physically, as in the places in the world you want to explore? No offense to Niagara Falls, but I'm dreaming bigger. I'm planning on trips to Paris, Rome, and recently I've become obsessed with going to Egypt to shop the street markets and see the pyramids.

You'll probably want to get online for this because we need you to see what's possible. And don't let your present income reign you in. Put on your *future vision glasses* and dream. Oh, and one other thing—go out and get your passport, and I mean now! Your day is coming if you can dream about it vividly enough.

Where Do You Want to Go?

"Why" These Specific Places?

> *I think I'll do some surfing and see what places I want to get to eventually.*

Place Pictures Here

What EXPERIENCES do I want to
HAVE...

Maybe you want to scuba dive, skydive, swim with dolphins, or try going vegan for a month. Or have a giant luau in your backyard, or maybe eat French toast in a café in Paris on a rainy April morning.

Why are experiences so powerful? They can't be taken from you. They last forever in your mind long after most things have rusted away. And when you do them with people you love, it takes the relationship to another level. Hell, even if you barely like them it'll forge a bond unlike much else. (If you've ever been on a rollercoaster with a friend you know what I mean.)

And unlike things, it's harder to compare experiences. They are perfectly unique. Your personal experiences are something no one else can ever own.

It's a big world, bitches. There's a lot of cool shit to experience, so take your time and think this one over.

List Your Dream Experiences Here...

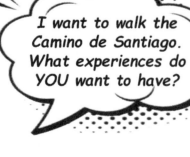

I want to walk the Camino de Santiago. What experiences do YOU want to have?

"Why" Do You Want This?

Place Pictures Here

What activities TRULY bring me
BLISS...

Besides pursuing your dream career, what other things bring you happiness? Joy? The things that put you in a state of absolute bliss? What are they for you?

Dancing? Singing? Running? Writing? Reading? Volunteering? Working in the garden, planting roses? I find my bliss through reading and, though I'm no Betty-fucking-Crocker, I LOVE baking. (I literally have dreams about swimming in a sea of cake batter, but let's save that for another time, shall we?)

Are there things you've stopped doing because you think you don't have the time? Well, fuck, if it brings you bliss, make time! I have six kids and I manage to do it. Give your soul a boost and remind it that life is more than drudgery. Do the things you love.

List the Things That Bring You Bliss Here...

For me, bliss is coaching my daughter's soccer team. What is it for _you_?

"Why" Do You Find Them Blissful?

Place Pictures Here

What is my CRAZIEST, MOST OUTRAGEOUS
DREAM...

I'm not talking about your job or career or house—I'm asking you about your craziest, most outrageous, the one you think of and then say, *"Oh, that could never happen."* Then you put it out of your mind because it seems impossible: *Go to Mars like Elon Musk? Remove all the plastic from the world's oceans? Circle the world in a hot air balloon? Feed one billion people?*

My crazy goal is to help put an end to sex trafficking. How am I going do it? Who the fuck knows? I start with *'what'* I want, and eventually the *'how'* is revealed.

So what is the outrageous thing *you* dream about? If you don't have one, get one. Everything starts with a dream.

Write Your Crazy Outrageous Dream Here...

"Why" Is This Important?

I'll tell you my craziest dreams if you tell me yours!

Place Pictures Here

What LEGACY do I want to

LEAVE...

Leaving a legacy is something most of use tend to think of once we have children, or perhaps after grandchildren arrive. By that time, it's often too late to put some of our legacy plans into action.

• Besides the obvious (which usually means money), what do you want to leave behind for the people who are important to you? And to the world?

• Who will you have mentored that pass on your knowledge to others even after they are gone?

• What works of art do you want to have left?

• In what ways do you want to have—in the words of Steve Jobs—left a 'dent' in the world?

And remember, the legacy you leave doesn't have to be in the form of money—it can be in any form.

Describe the Legacy
You Want to Leave...

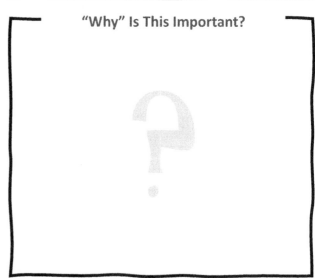

"Why" Is This Important?

Here Lies
Branden LaNette
She spent her life inspiring others to love themselves and received an ocean of love in return.

Place Pictures Here

To get everything I want, how much $$$ do I need to
MAKE...

Thought this would come first, didn't you?

Yes, making lots of money is important—the world runs on money. But ultimately most people discover what they really wanted all along was freedom and to feel good about themselves. So don't make it your master, because if you have to make it in a way that goes against your values, doing work you hate with people you can't stand—it can also become a cage.

That said: how much do you need to make to afford the life you want? What is your best guess? Better still, why not research the cost of the things you've described in this workbook?

• *How much does your dream house cost?*

• *What is the mortgage payment at todays current interest rate?*

• *How much is your dream car?*

• *What would be needed to pay for a 10-day, first-class trip to your dream destination?*

Do you know how much you need to earn to fund your dream life? You should. After all, if you don't know the details, then you're just *dreaming* about it, and not really planning for it.

P.S. Money isn't everything, but it fucking helps.

Insert Your Answers Here

Per Week?

Per Year?

In Your Account?

This page is designed
to be cut out and put
in an8: x 10" frame.
Just cut on the
dotted lines on the
opposite side.

PART IV:

What Are You Willing to Do to Get It?

I'm ready to work my ass off and take some risks because I've been playing it safe for way too long!

What SKILLS do I need to
ACQUIRE...

It's nice to think each of us has all the skills we need to make our dreams come true; that all we have to do is apply them. Unfortunately, the further we move down the path toward our dreams, the more we realize we need to learn. It's a never-ending cycle.

What Do You Need to Learn?

But, hey, the best life is one in which we are constantly learning, so *learning how much we still need to learn* is a good thing.

The more we tend to learn

The more we realize there's more to know

So what things do you need to learn? What skills do you need to develop? What gaps in ability do you have? Talent is something we're born with, but skills are something we need to earn.

Make a list!

If my dream is to do business with China, it might be a good idea to learn some Chinese. And there's a course right here!

What BOOKS do I want/need to
READ...

Interviews with 1,200 of the world's richest people discovered the one thing virtually all of them had in common. And that thing? They were voracious readers. Walk into any wealthy person's home and what do you almost always find? An extensive library. And what kind of books are in these libraries? Romance novels? No. (I like a good romance novel as much as the next girl, but escapism won't get you a dream life.)

But we know this already, don't we? We know education is the foundation of success, and that *readers are leaders.* So why don't we read more? Don't say you lack time, bitches. We've all got the time—we simply don't make reading the priority it needs to be. Right now I'm busier than shit and still finding time to read *Breaking the Habit of Being Yourself* (which I highly recommend.)

So, read, damnit!

Bye-bye, Netflix—hello, dreams!

What am I going to do to get the most from

TIME...

The one thing we know for sure is that, when we reach the end of life, every one of us will wish for more of one thing and one thing only: *time.* Money won't matter. Awards? Cars? Seriously? No, all we'll want is one more day, one more hour, one more minute of life. Yet time is the thing we waste most.

If you live an average length life, you'll be on Earth approximately 81 years, which is 29,585 days, or 709,560 hours. How can you get the most out of those hours? My suggestion is to spend at least 10 minutes every day working on the exercises in this fucking workbook. That will keep you focused on what you want to achieve in those precious hours and keep you in action moving toward your goals and dreams.

Make Your List Here

I've wasted a shitload of time already—but not anymore!

This page is designed
to be cut out and put
in an8: x 10" frame.
Just cut on the
dotted lines on the
opposite side.

What VALUES do I need to
EMBODY...

If you were able to see a time lapse movie of one year in someone's life, you'd be able to determine many of their values based on what they did.

When faced with a choice, it's going to be your VALUES that dictate which you choose. For example, you are still in bed at 8 am on Sunday morning, and church starts at 9 am. If your faith is one of your highest values, you drag your ass out of bed and go.

With that as an example, think about your values, bitches. What values do you have now? Which do you want to cultivate? *Authenticity? Family? Honesty? Community? Spirituality? Compassion? Ambition? Hard work? Contribution? Personal Growth? Self-Reliance?*

Ask yourself if your values are in alignment with your goals. If they are, great. But if they aren't…

Make Your List Here

Values are important. I should take the time to outline the values I want to embody!

Who can I use as TEACHERS and
MENTORS...

Make Your List Here

You hear the term "mentor" thrown about a lot and the reason is simple. It's important, bitches. But what the hell is a mentor, exactly? Think of a mentor as a person who acts as a kind of "adviser, counselor, teacher, trainer, coach, guide…" you get the idea.

"But, Branden, I can't find anyone to mentor me!"
You can't find a mentor? WTF?

Let me tell you about a secret place I discovered where there are thousands of mentors—it's called YouTube. You may know of it. There is more information available for FREE on YouTube right now than used to exist in all the libraries in the world—and you don't even have to drive. Fuck, you don't even have to get dressed! And though I hate to sound morbid, most of my best mentors are dead—people like Zig Ziglar, Jim Rohn, and Kobe Bryant who just left us as this workbook was being written.

So, who are yours going to be?

Don't tell anyone, but I've got a bit of a crush on Elon Musk!

Who has SKILLS I want to EMULATE...

The next question is: Who do you admire? And why? What is about them that you wish to emulate? Their work ethic? Their perfectionism? Their creativity? What makes them worthy of your admiration?

Some of these people may be the mentors you've already identified. Others may be people you admire for a singular reason. For example, I strive to emulate Beyoncé, not for her singing and dancing (which is amazing and stuff I could never come close to doing) but for her outrageous work ethic. I also admire Reese Witherspoon and Oprah for their love of books and what they've done to promote reading.

Find at least 10 such people whose skills or traits you'd like to emulate and write them in the box on this page, along with the trait (or traits) you wish to emulate. Then find their pictures on the internet and paste them in the boxes.

I want to emulate Sara Blakley because she's one bold and courageous bitch!

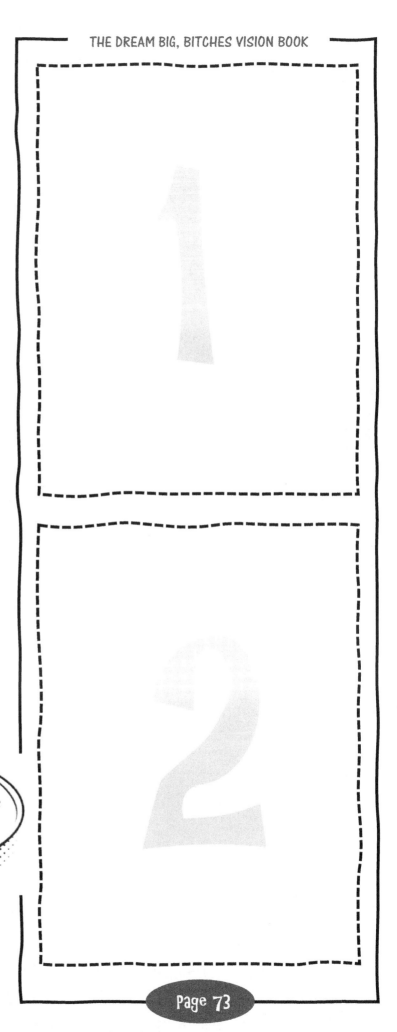

3

4

5

6

7

8

9

10

How can I take advantage of my
STRENGTHS...

Everyone has at least one "Oprah-level" strength—something they are outrageously skilled at—that can be leveraged in the marketplace. It may be something they're a "natural" at like singing, being 7'2" tall, or having a great sense of humor. (Can you spell Jim Carrey?) Then again, it may be something learned like sales and negotiation skills or computer coding. Add to that, everyone on the planet has at least one unique quality. In my case, that unique quality happens to be my tattoos (see book cover for living proof.)

So, what are your biggest strengths, natural or learned? And what is it that makes you unique?

If you need some examples to get you started, check out the list of strengths on the next page. But don't limit yourself to this list—it is just there to get you thinking. And don't forget your unique traits; everyone as at least one, and maybe many. Ask other people for help with this if you want. They may have more objectivity.

List Your Six Greatest Strengths and/or Unique Qualities Here...

1

2

3

4

5

6

VARIOUS STRENGTHS TO CONSIDER

Problem Solving	High Integrity
Logical	Open-Minded
Self-Motivated	Resourceful
Ambitious	Diplomatic
Dedicated	Generous
Patient	Caring
Organized	Creative/Artistic
Proactive	Persistent
Independent	Spiritual
Detail Oriented	Humble
Trustworthy	Responsible
Unselfish	Good Listener
Considerate	Courageous
Analytical	Authentic
Optimistic	Kind
Inspiring	Loving
Enthusiastic	Perceptive
Flexible	Funny

What are my HIGH IMPACT DOMINOS...

What are "High Impact Dominos?" Well, there are two types, so let me tell you about each:

Example #1... <u>BIG</u> Dominos that automatically knock many other dominos down. Say you want to live in Portland in the summer, and Orlando in the winter (duh!) Here's the thing: the best way to get *both* is to focus on *neither*. Instead, focus on the domino of starting a profitable home business that allows you to buy multiple houses and live anywhere you want.

Example #2... <u>SMALL</u> Dominos with huge long-term impact, like putting $200 into an IRA account that, 30 years later (through the magic of compound interest) will add up to a big amount that will help you achieve many other goals. Identify at least three:

List 3 'High Impact Dominos' Here...

1

2

3

> You mean that if I topple this one domino down, all the rest go down automatically? Holy shit!

PART V:

What Are You Willing To Stop Doing?

> Okay, I admit it, I spend a crap-ton of time surfing the internet. I know I can cut back on some of that!

Removing "Restrainers" vs. Hitting the Gas

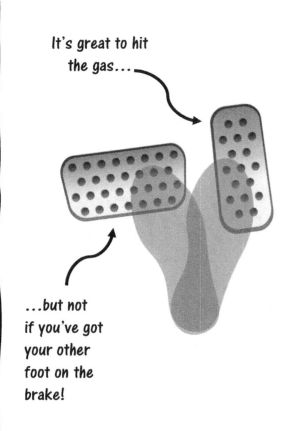

It's great to hit the gas...

...but not if you've got your other foot on the brake!

No wonder I'm not getting anywhere—I've still got my foot on my performance brake!

There are basically two ways a person can move a vehicle forward (without getting out and pushing, that is):

1. **The <u>first</u> way is obvious: put your foot <u>on</u> the gas.**

2. **The <u>second</u> is not so obvious, which is by taking your foot <u>off</u> the brake.**

The problem for most people is they spend the majority of their time learning new skills to accelerate performance—in other words, *hitting the gas.* However, they often find themselves disappointed when the results they were seeking fail to appear.

The reason…

While they were focused on hitting the gas, *they forgot to take their other foot off the brake!* The engine is revving like mad, but they're spinning their wheels and going nowhere fast.

On the other hand, if they'd had simply taken their foot off the brake, they'd have moved forward.

The following pages are designed to help you with ways to take your foot off your brake.

If you don't, you'll never move forward.

What BAD HABITS am I willing to
ELIMINATE...

Make Your List Here

Michelangelo carved his famous statue of David from a single block of unwanted marble that had twice been discarded by other artists. It was simply too big, and too daunting a task. When it was unveiled in 1501, people were in awe of the achievement. *"How ever did you do it?"* people asked in amazement, to which Michelangelo responded, *"Fuck if I know."* Actually, what he said was a lot cooler: he said, *"All I did was to imagine what the statue would look like when it was finished, then chipped away everything that wasn't David."*

What bad habits do *you* have? Things that, if you chipped them away, the best version of yourself would be revealed? I admit to having Tee Many Martoonies from time to time and spending an ungodly amount of time on TikTok. What about you? The first step to removing bad habits is to admit you have them, bitches—*and you know you do.*

I have a choice— abandon my bad habits or abandon my dreams!

What UNUSED shit am I willing to
GET RID OF...

Make Your List Here

I've never been your house, and yet I can say with a high degree of certainty that you have a lot of shit you don't need. What kind of shit? Let's start with coffee mugs, stolen (I mean permanently borrowed) pens, clocks, decorative figurines, magazines, unread books, CDs and DVDs which no human really needs anymore, a guitar you haven't played since high school, clothes you've been planning to get into for 10 years now, 16 extension cords, worn-out running shoes, an unused broken rowing machine, do-it-yourself ice cream maker, a stack of take-out menus from restaurants (many which are out of business) and so many plastic bags you need a plastic bag to keep them in (which is probably in a box) and I haven't even gotten to the garage yet. This shit has got to go!

If you haven't read *The Life-Changing Magic of Tidying Up*, by Marie Kondo, do asap. And then, when you're done reading it and doing what she recommends, donate it—along with everything else.

Eliminating clutter makes room for treasures!

What UNNECESARY SHIT am I willing to
STOP BUYING...

Make Your List Here

I really like to buy shit, and I imagine you do, too. But a lot of the things I buy I get just because I want them (rather than need them) or I think they'll impress my friends, family , co-workers, (ugh!) or strangers. There's nothing worse than wasting money on trying to impress people who could not care less about us, especially when we should be using that money to move closer to our real dreams.

Enough with stuff, okay? Stop spending and start investing. Time is money, but money is also time. Every time you buy something you really don't need, don't think of it as *money* spent, but as *time* spent. Next time you're tempted to buy a pair of shoes, ask yourself, *"How many <u>hours</u> do these cost?"* It helps put things in perspective, doesn't it?

I knew there had to be a catch! Just don't tell me I've got to stop buying shoes!

Which RELATIONSHIPS am I willing to
CURTAIL...

The dictionary says the word curtail means to "reduce in extent or quantity; impose a restriction on; to deprive someone of." Let me use it in a sentence: *I can guarantee you have relationships you need to seriously fucking curtail right now.*

If you read *Once Upon a Time, Bitches,* you might remember I highly encouraged you to kick toxic people out of your life. That's still my advice. But if your ex or your toxic sister-in-law wants to come over for Thanksgiving, you need to *curtail* that shit.

There is nothing that will bring you down faster than negative people. They don't care about your success, and probably enjoy making you miserable.

As Maya Angelou said, *"Don't bring negative to my door."* You can always count on Maya for good advice.

Relationships I Need to "Curtail"...

Attention, everyone: If you're not positive and support my dreams, I'll still let you come over, but you aren't staying long!

What DISTRACTIONS do I need to
REMOVE...

Sometimes it feels like everyone and everything needs your attention—I know, I have six kids, a plethora of pets, and a husband who comes home hungry and horny. So, how and when does *my* work get done? The answer, of course, is *'before, after, and in between.'* And the last thing I need are unwanted distractions.

Researchers at the University of California, Irvine, found it takes people as long as 25 minutes to return to the task they were doing after being interrupted or distracted. That's a fuck ton of lost time.

Make a list of the things that typically distract you (TV, cell phones ringing, social media, etc.) and vow to remove as many of them as possible when you're trying to be productive.

Make Your List Here

> *Okay, I'm onboard as long as you don't consider shopping a distraction!*

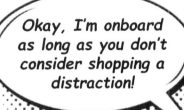

What REGRETS do I want to make sure to
AVOID...

Make Your "Potential Regrets" List Here

Most of us fear reaching the end of life and finding ourselves and thinking:

- *Shit, I wish I'd spent more time with my friends and my family.*

- *Fuck, I wish I'd taken better care of my health when I had the chance.*

- *Damn, I wish I'd listened to my inner voice more.*

- *I wish I'd told (fill in the blank) I loved them.*

- *Why in the fuck did I spend so much time with my loser friends?*

- *What could I have achieved if I didn't give a shit about what other people thought of me?*

- *I wish I'd trusted myself more.*

- *I wish I'd pursued my dream instead of taking the safe, practical job my parents wanted me to take.*

Notice all the swearing? Trust me, when you get to the final few hours of your life and reflect on all the shit you didn't do, you could end up swearing a lot.

So, what might *you* find yourself regretting? Better figure it out now, before it's too late.

I wish life had a rewind button!

What WHINING & COMPLAINING do I need to

DUMP...

Make Your List Here

I'm not talking about the stupid shit we say silently to ourselves in our head (and maybe sometimes out loud)—I'm talking about the stupid, negative, whiny-shit we talk about with other people. You know what I'm talking about…

- *My boss/job sucks…*
- *It's too damn hot/cold outside…*
- *I hate the Kardashians…*
- *My husband leaves the toilet seat up…*
- *God, I'm so hungover…*
- *The prices for food are skyrocketing…*

Value delivered? *Zero.* Damage created? *Significant.*

So stop complaining already! It makes you sound angry and dumb, and it's bad for everyone else around you. Be honest and write down 10 things you complain about a lot, and then knock that shit off!

Which of my GOALS am I willing to
DITCH...

Wait, Branden, I thought this was a goal setting book. Now you're saying I need to ditch some of my goals? What gives? I don't get it.

The point of setting goals is to give ourselves a direction to move in, and that's good. But…

Too Many Goals = Too Many Directions.
Too Many Directions = Too Many Distractions.
Too Many Distractions = Not Achieving Your Goals.

My ONE BIG GOAL is to be a writer, and it's working out. But what if I also wanted to be a singer, a chiropractor, a dog trainer, and an Olympic athlete? The truth is, you can have anything you want, *but you just can't have everything you want*. What goals are you willing to ditch? Make a list and let them go.

> I'm way too scattered. I won't let my goals work against me!

Goals that are Getting in the Way of My "Goals"…

PART VI:

Identifying Self-Limiting Beliefs

> We are here on this planet only once, and to limit that experience with a head full of bullshit beliefs is a crime!

What LIMITING BELIEFS do I need to
SURRENDER?

Limiting beliefs are what they sound like: beliefs that limit your ability to achieve your dreams, often lurking below the surface of your consciousness like the unseen part of an iceberg, just waiting to sink your dreams. And overcoming them isn't easy. I was raised being told that rich people were greedy, and that belief has taken years to shake. You need to develop awareness that you have them, catch yourself when one enters your mind, and then remind yourself that the belief is 100% made-up bullshit.

At every turn, ask yourself: *"Does this belief serve me? Will having this belief help me achieve my dreams? Is this belief even true?"* Also ask yourself, *"What are the long-term consequences of maintaining this belief?"*

We put labels on ourselves, and then we become a slave to those labels. Identifying your limiting beliefs is challenging, but it's worth it.

Decisions, Actions, Behaviors

The sea of self-limiting beliefs that keep you from achieving your dreams, often hidden below the surface

You're too old...
You'll never be rich...
Doing what you love is selfish...
You have no self discipline...
Blah, fucking, blah!

BELIEFS

- ❑ Everyone else wins, but I never will.
- ❑ There's not enough to go around.
- ❑ Earning money requires a high IQ.
- ❑ Money is the root of all evil
- ❑ Money doesn't grow on trees
- ❑ I don't want to pay big taxes.
- ❑ I am bad with money I always waste it.
- ❑ I will never be rich.
- ❑ Rich people are bad people.
- ❑ People with money can't be trusted.
- ❑ Money isn't important to me.
- ❑ The rich get rich, and the poor get poorer.
- ❑ Getting rich requires selling your soul.
- ❑ The world is a cruel, mean place.
- ❑ I can't get rich without a college degree.
- ❑ I'll never find love, I'm not worthy.
- ❑ My relationships never seem to work out.
- ❑ I can't be happy unless I have a partner.
- ❑ I need someone to take care of me.
- ❑ Love always ends up with getting hurt.
- ❑ There's no point in dreaming, I'll never make it.
- ❑ I am not enough on my own.
- ❑ The world is out to get me/keep me down.
- ❑ Doing what I love is selfish.
- ❑ I'm obligated to do what my parents want.
- ❑ Rejection is the worst thing in the world.
- ❑ You can't make money doing work you love.
- ❑ Rich people have no integrity.
- ❑ I don't have the talent to be successful.
- ❑ My looks are the reason I'm not successful.
- ❑ There's no reason to try, I'll just fail.
- ❑ My opinions aren't important.

- ❑ Losing weight is an impossible battle.
- ❑ I lack the money/resources to succeed.
- ❑ I'm too young/old to be successful/accepted.
- ❑ I'm not connected enough to succeed.
- ❑ Other people are standing in my way.
- ❑ It's too early to start, I'm not ready.
- ❑ Work is not supposed to be enjoyable.
- ❑ I don't deserve to have a wonderful life.
- ❑ Rich people inherit their money, it's not fair.
- ❑ I don't have enough time/energy to succeed.
- ❑ It's too late to start taking care of my body.
- ❑ Financial security is for other people, not me.
- ❑ One of these day I'll get motivated and change.
- ❑ Getting my hopes up leads to disappointment.
- ❑ I can't do more, my plate is too full already.
- ❑ I'm too old to change.
- ❑ People won't like me if I'm too successful.
- ❑ Failure is inevitable, it's better not to try.
- ❑ Eating healthy is too much work.
- ❑ Life is hard, there's no getting around it.
- ❑ I need others' approval to feel happy/worthy.
- ❑ I'll always be broke, being poor is my destiny.
- ❑ I'm not self-disciplined.
- ❑ There's no point in asking for what I want.
- ❑ It's hopeless, I'm powerless to succeed.
- ❑ I wasn't born into the right family.

I don't want to cling to false limitations anymore! What about you?

What BULLSHIT STORIES do I need to STOP TELLING MYSELF?

If you love movies, you know the power they have to move us and stir emotions. This is because writers and directors know what they're doing—they've harnessed the *power of storytelling.*

We also have movies that play on the movie screen in our mind—short little subconscious films that have the power to control our emotions and shape our future reality. And who writes and directs these internal little movies? *We do, bitches!* If you want a better future, you've got to tell yourself better stories—stories where you star as the hero and victor, not the villain or victim— you've got to tell yourself better stories.

People say, *"Well, the past is the past, there's nothing I can do about it."* True, and yet, not true. Yes, whatever happened, happened. The past can't be changed, but how you think about it *can* be.

So, ask yourself, "W*hat stories do I keep telling myself? And how can I change them to make them more empowering?* Then start telling yourself *new stories* with better endings.

EXERCISE / PART I: List at least four (4) limiting stories you keep telling yourself (for example, *"My parents worked all the time, which means they didn't love me. That's proof that I am unlovable."*

Limiting Story

#1...

Limiting Story

#2...

Limiting Story

#3...

Limiting Story

#4...

PART II: For each Limiting Story you've identified, re-write them to be empowering (for example, *"My parents worked long hours to provide for me, which is proof they loved me!"*

Empowering Story

#1...

Empowering Story

#2...

Empowering Story

#3...

Empowering Story

#4...

PART VII:

Operating From a Place of Gratitude

This is going to be super easy. I've got a lot of things to be grateful for!

For what am I most
GRATEFUL...

Make Your List Here

There are few tools more powerful than gratitude, especially when life becomes challenging. I am always amazed at how uplifted and *centered* I become when I turn my attention to the positive aspects of my life.

So, if you've never done it before, take some time and make a list of everything in your life for which you are grateful, including people, possessions, skills, experiences, freedom, the sun, the earth, and on and on. And, while you're at it, how about taking some time to simply being grateful for the "life force energy" that runs through you and makes life possible?

Drown yourself in gratitude for everything that's happened to you in your life, good or bad. If you take nothing else from this workbook, remember to be grateful. Be fucking grateful for it all.

> *The first step in getting what you want is appreciating what you've already got.*

WHO AM I GRATEFUL FOR?

Place Pictures Here

WHO AM I GRATEFUL FOR?

Place Pictures Here

BRANDEN LANETTE

WHAT AM I GRATEFUL FOR?

Place Pictures Here

WHAT AM I GRATEFUL FOR?

Place Pictures Here

BRANDEN LANETTE

Okay, Let's Wrap This Puppy...

Congratulations, you did the work!

Or did you? Dear God, bitches, I hope you're not reading this having flipped though the entire workbook without writing out what you want and putting visuals next to them. The thought of that makes me want to cry. So if you didn't do the work, I'm going to pretend you did.

The Formula for Success

I've long wondered if there really is a formula for success. A simple one. Not some complex, 107-step bullshit diagram that no one could possibly understand let alone execute. And I believe there is.

And here it is:

1. DECIDE WHAT YOU WANT.

2. DETERMINE THE PRICE.

3. FUCKING PAY IT.

ANYTHING BEYOND THIS IS JUST COMPLICATION.

The key to our success lay in our willingness to decide what we want, to figure out the steps we we need to take to get it, *and then to do the work,* even when we don't feel like it. Complicate the process if you want, but why would you?

The only limitations to what you can achieve are your limiting beliefs, so ditch that shit!

You are in control of your thoughts and your actions. *You.* No one else. Just you. So, get control of your thoughts, keep your dreams in front of you, and then just do the work. *Do the fucking work.*

Love,

Branden

About the Author...

BRANDEN LANETTE doesn't look like a typical author, but she has long ignored what she "should" do, say and look like. On her own at a very young age, Branden eventually found herself with the wrong guy, the wrong job, and a bleak future. The fairytale she was promised as a child never materialized.

Finally, Branden decided that she wanted something different for her life and realized no one was going to do it for her. Prince charming wasn't coming to save her—she'd have to save herself.

Step by step, decision by decision, through major trials and tribulations that would stop most people in their tracks, Branden learned how to turn heartbreak into happiness <u>and</u> self-judgement into inner joy.

Today, Branden LaNette is an entrepreneur, coach, speaker, wife, and stay-at-home Mom to six C-section babies (ages 2-17) and way too many f-ing pets. Somehow, however, she manages to juggle all of this effortlessly (a blatant lie) while pushing her way through the kinds of fear and self-doubts that whisper within all of us (totally true) to achieve her goals. Her most recent dream come true is this book, one that is destined to have a major impact on millions of women across the globe (or at least nine people in Michigan.)

Through it all, she has found her happiness, her joy— *and her unique voice.*

Let's Connect, Bitches!

Oh, and don't forget, visit me at: **OnceUponATimeBitches.com**

Finally, thank you so much for taking this journey with me. You are part of my dream come true.

Is now an okay time to ask for a favor? I would LOVE and greatly appreciate if you would consider leaving an honest review of my book on your favorite book buying platform.

 Facebook: Branden.Lanette

 Instagram: @Brandenlanettel

 Twitter: @Branden_LaNette

Hey, get my other book!

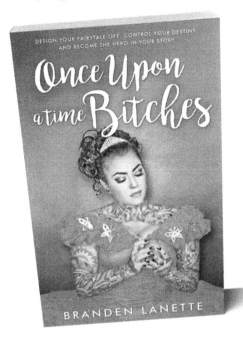

Hi, I'm Branden. That is me on the cover. Yes, I have a boy's name, a Mom bod, and the tattoos are not photoshopped. Once upon a time I realized we all have a story, we all have a struggle and happiness is relative. I am not cynical or hardened, I am just stating the facts. Here's the deal:

- *Prince Charming doesn't exist.*
- *Fairy Godmother is drunk.*
- *Glass slippers don't come with 2-day free prime shipping from Amazon.*

There is no magic fairytale, but if <u>YOU</u> work at it enough you can come pretty close creating your version with a happy ending. The best part is, in life you can continue to make edits until that sh*t reads exactly how you want it to.

You may not agree with everything I say in this book, but the most important takeaway is that YOU have to be your own hero. No more damsel locked in a tower, bullsh*t.

That ends now. Join me as I take you through my 7 Magical Maxims for creating a fairytale life. (I know what you are thinking: Branden, no one gets a fairytale life.) Can you stop being so damn cynical for two seconds and just go with this? Good. Here they are:

> <u>Maxim #1</u> Realize that no one is coming to save you. You have to save yourself.
>
> <u>Maxim #2</u>: Accept total responsibility for every damn aspect of your life.
>
> <u>Maxim #3</u>: Stop comparing yourself to others and just f*cking be you.
>
> <u>Maxim #4</u>: Dream dreams that are so big they make people doubt you.
>
> <u>Maxim #5</u>: Your life is the sum of your choices. Choose well.
>
> <u>Maxim #6</u>: Eliminate everything evil and negative from your kingdom.
>
> <u>Maxim #7</u>: Love yourself so hard you have an abundance to share with others.

Is it possible to design a fairytale life? Control your destiny? Be the hero in your story? I believe you can and that's why I wrote this book. I am going to make you a little uncomfortable. Back out now if you aren't ready, because sh*t's about to get real, bitches!

> <u>Note</u>: Do to limited space, I didn't go into the importance of affirmations. If you're interested seeing the affirmations I use, you can download them at:
>
> **www.BrandenLaNette.com/Affirmations**

Hey, you read Branden's other book, is it any good?

And you didn't get me one?

Yeah, I loved it so much ! Bought copies for all my friends!

Oops!

This page is designed
to be cut out and put
in an8: x 10" frame.
Just cut on the
dotted lines on the
opposite side.

IGNORE THE HATERS & THE TROLLS.

LIVE THE LIFE YOU FUCKING WANT TO LIVE!

-Branden LaNette
OnceUponATimeBitches.com

This page is designed
to be cut out and put
in an8: x 10" frame.
Just cut on the
dotted lines on the
opposite side.

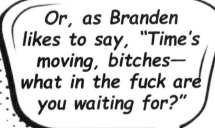

Made in the USA
Monee, IL
16 December 2020